so you want to be a want to be a worshipper

Worship Redefined

GAIL FLY

Limits of Liability and Disclaimer of Warranty
The author and publisher shall not be liable for your misuse of this material. This book is strictly for informational purposes.
The purpose of this book is to educate and entertain. The author and publisher do not guarantee anyone following these techniques, suggestions, tips, ideas, or strategies will
become successful. The author and publisher shall have neither liability nor responsibility to anyone with respect to any loss or damage caused, or alleged to be caused, directly or indirectly by the information contained in this book. Views expressed in this publication do not necessarily reflect the views of the publisher.

Printed in the United States of America

Keen Vision Publishing, LLC
www.keen-vision.com
ISBN 978-1-948270-38-0

Contents

Introduction

Picture this. It's Sunday morning. You walk into your church, take your seat, and wait for service to begin. Service starts, and when it's time for praise and worship, no one shows up. The band doesn't play. The praise team nor choir mounts the platform. No one prompts us to clap our hands, lift our voices, or stand to our feet. What would praise and worship look like then? Would it even exist? Would we still call it praise and worship?

Praise is what we do, say, or give in exchange for something done. We praise our children for doing well in school. We praise the success of others. It is an expressed emotion for something done. When we praise God, we show our appreciation for what He has done. If you receive a gift, your natural, uncoerced, and automatic response would be *thank you*. It should be the same when God does anything for you. God's blessings warrant a "thank you." Praise is how we thank God for what He has done for us. It has nothing to do with our relationship with Him. Praise is for everybody.

Worship, on the other hand, has nothing to do with what God does for you. We worship God because of

God. It is about what we give to God. Think about this. If you didn't have the car, *who would God be to you?* If you couldn't close on the house, *what would God mean to you?* If you didn't get the job you prayed for, *what would your worship look like?* Worship has taken on various forms in the church. While it may look different depending on the assembly we attend, the foundation of worship remains the same; the Bible is still right. To worship God, we must do so in Spirit and in Truth, according to St. John 4:24. We cannot worship God without having a relationship with Him. It is impossible to truly worship what we do not know.

In addition to helping worshippers gain a solid foundation of why and how we worship, the purpose of this book is to challenge worshippers to speak against the parades of the flesh in the house of God in the name of worship. If we don't speak against it, we are just as guilty of it. Upon reading this, many may respond with an often misused scripture and say we should not judge. However, Matthew 7:1 (NKJV) says, *"Judge not that ye be not judged."*

This verse means that we shouldn't judge unless we want to be judged. The only person who does not want to be judged (by the Word of God) is the person whose life does not align with it. Am I saying that makes any one of us perfect? If we use the true meaning of perfect, being mature, then *yes.* If we define perfection as being without flaw, then absolutely not.

So You Want to Be A Worshipper is not designed to ridicule worshippers, but rather to challenge us to examine

examine our lives and live what we sing, lead, or instruct others to do in service. We can't worship a Holy God in sin. No longer can we stand by and allow our altars, choir stands, and pulpits to be stained. The time has come for worshippers to realign ourselves with the standard of holiness and give God the pure worship that is due to Him.

Chapter One

In Spirit and Truth

Webster defines worship as *honoring or respecting someone or something as a god.* With this definition, whatever or whoever you worship can be your god – *small g.* To worship God, the supreme being, the all-knowing and infinite Spirit; one must know Him. You cannot worship what you have not come to know. St. John 4:24 (KJV) tells us, *"God is a Spirit: and they that worship Him must worship Him in spirit and in truth."* The New King James Version says, *"God is Spirit, and those who worship Him must worship in spirit and truth."* The scripture interpretations are almost identical, and the context is the same: *God is a Spirit, and if we're going to worship Him we must do so in spirit and truth.*

Spirit is defined as the immaterial, intelligent, or sentient (aware or finely sensitive) part of a person. To worship God in spirit goes beyond what we do physically. It is beyond the words we sing and the movement of our bodies. Our ability to worship in spirit depends upon the posture of our hearts rather than our bodies. It is possible to lay prostrate in sin. It is possible to sing praises and still be full of pride. It is possible to lead praise and worship and still be rude, hateful, and lack integrity. However, when we worship God in spirit, our thoughts, attitudes, and actions must be submitted to God.

Truth is pretty self-explanatory. We worship God in the truth of who we are, the truth of where we are in life, and the truth of who God is to us. Worship is not based upon what we need or what we are going through. We worship in the greatest truth: *The truth of who God is.*

Worshipping God in spirit and truth are not two separate occasions. Despite the many ways we may worship, we must worship in spirit and in truth simultaneously. The worship that God requires of us is costly and will require us to make some sacrifices. True worship can only happen at the expense of the things we think we need, our attitudes, our will, our heartbreak, separation, and habits and beliefs we hold near and dear.

Though the word *worshipper* is thrown around loosely, the Bible tells us exactly what God accepts as true worship. It's impossible to call ourselves worshippers without fulfilling the requirements of worship outlined in St. John 4:24. What makes one a worshipper is first their acknowledgment and recognition of who God is. You cannot worship what you do not know. Once we acknowledge God for who He is, we must surrender our will to His.

While John 4:24 shows us how God desires us to worship Him, the first scripture reference of worship is found in Genesis 22. God calls Abraham and he answers. God tells him to take his son, Isaac, to the land of Moriah and offer him as a burnt offering. Verse 3 tells us that Abraham rose early the next morning and prepared for his journey to Moriah. He took two travelers along with him for the trip. As they approach the place where the sacrifice would take place, Abraham tells the young men who traveled with him to stay with the donkey. He says to them in Genesis 22:5 (KJV), *"I and the lad will go yonder and worship, and come again to you."* Later, as Abraham is about to sacrifice his son to God, an angel appeared and stopped Abraham. God provided a ram for Abraham to offer as a sacrifice and his son lived.

In order to pull the revelation from this passage, we must keep in mind the story of Abraham and his wife, Sarah. They prayed for a child for much of their marriage, and in their old age, God blessed them with a son whom they named Issac. Then, God instructs Abraham to offer the son He gave them as a sacrifice on a mountain that God would reveal to him. Though those instructions seemed cruel and made very little sense, Abraham obeyed God. Abraham had a real relationship with God. He knew who God was and trusted Him.

Who hearkens to the voice of God when the instructions make no sense at all? *Worshippers!* Abraham did not question how, what, and when. He obeyed the instructions of God. He put Isaac on the altar, on the mountain God told him to go to, in the land God told him to travel to. In verse five, Abraham called what he was about to do *worship*. This shows us that we can't be worshippers and be disobedient to God. Being a worshipper requires our obedience even when it doesn't make sense to us. Worship can only be worship when we move, live, and operate in obedience to God.

It's sad, but many of the clichés we say in church make us overlook the importance of being obedient to God. While we should fully acknowledge the scripture that admonishes us to *"speak those things that be not as though they were,"* (Romans 4:17b), we also must understand that there are some things we will never obtain until we are obedient to God. In the midst of yelling, *"Say it till you see it! Call it and haul it! See it and seize it! Have it and grab it! Turn around three times and say I got it!"* we must understand that many of the promises of God are convenants that require something from us. In order for us to have what God says we can have, we must walk in obedience to His word. We can't cling to cute church clichés and think we're going to see manifestation when we're living contrary to God's word. It doesn't work that way. We can absolutely say it till we see it, when we are saying what God is saying and living how God wants us to live. We can't live however we want to live and do whatever we want to do and expect God to bless us. God has an order that we must obey if we want to be blessed.

It is hard to encourage people to obey God if we are not obeying God. As worshippers, we must ask ourselves, *Am I living in obedience to God and His word?* No one can answer this question for us, so we must be honest with ourselves. There's no need to lie because God already knows the truth. Take inventory of your life, heart, intentions, and motives. Have you been obedient to God? When the Holy Spirit led me to write this, I wasn't sure if it would be a book, pamphlet, or webinar. As I developed this work, it forced me to take inventory of my level of obedience. As praise and worship leaders, we must stop performing and parading our flesh in His house and calling it worship. Despite how it moves onlookers, worshippers will be held accountable for not living up to the standards of true worship.

Many of us know that some of our brothers and sisters are living in direct contradiction to the word of God, yet we still sing behind them in churches all across state lines. Even though they have a good sound and their gift opens doors, we must get to a place where we desire to be in right standing with God more than we desire success and accolades. It should scare us to sing for the nation knowing that our lives are not aligned with what we sing about. One day, we will die. It will be sad to have spent our days singing and praising God though we never knew Him or heeded His words. Mark 8:37 poses a question I believe every worshipper should consider, *"Or what shall a man give in exchange for his soul?"* (KJV) So, what makes you a worshipper? Is it the opportunities you've been granted? The social media flyers you've been featured on? The money pastors and ministries have paid you to open their services? The EP's you've released? The big events you've headlined? Your number of followers? *No!* None of these things make us worshippers. What makes us worshippers is not our ability to move the crowd, but our ability to worship God in spirit and in truth.

Take a moment and reflect on your life as a worshipper. Answer the following questions honestly.

Aside from how He has blessed you, what do you know about God?

_____

_____

_____

_____

_____

_____

_____

_____

_____

_____

_____

_____

_____

_____

_____

_____

_____

_____

What changes are you willing to make to ensure your life is aligned with the Word of God?

_____

_____

_____

_____

_____

_____

_____

_____

_____

What have you allowed to identify you as a worshipper?

_____

_____

_____

_____

_____

_____

_____

_____

_____

After reading this chapter, what changes will you make in your life to ensure that you meet God's standard for being a true worshipper?

_____

_____

_____

_____

_____

_____

_____

_____

_____

_____

_____

_____

_____

_____

_____

_____

_____

_____

_____

_____

Chapter Two

The Power of the Tongue

What are you saying? Not literally, but in your heart? What consumes your thoughts? The Bible tells us in Matthew 12:34 that out of the abundance of our hearts, our mouths speak. Being created in God's image gives us the authority to create and frame our worlds by the words we release from our mouths. As worshippers, it is vital that our speech matches our declarations. It's easy to stand before a multitude and make declarations we have either heard or read, but do we believe them? A quote by Samuel Taylor Coleridge says, *"What comes from the heart, goes to the heart."* When a person is sincere, genuine, pure, and authentic, you can feel it, and it is easy to receive. The same should be for your worship. If you are a worshipper, we should feel *something* when you stand before the people to lead praise and worship. There should be a shifting – *a moving from one place to the next.* The response may not always be the same. It may not be tears or brokenness all the time, but there should be some sort of connection from you to God and from you to those in the audience. You can't be a worshipper and your heart not be touched by your own worship to God. *If you don't feel it, how will anyone else?*

Your spoken decrees and declarations during worship should match your lifestyle – *away from the house of God.* You must communicate with God outside of praise and worship on Sunday morning. That portion of the service is not the summation of worship; it's the designated time for us to worship corporately. Individual and private worship are mandatory for every worship leader. Many times, this is the reason there is no response or participation from the audience when we lead praise and worship. The audience does not have to stand, clap, cry, scream, dance, or fall out for it to be worship. However, when a real worshipper stands in obedience and honor to God to lead people in worship, a connection will be felt. There will be a response. In many churches, worship leaders are cheerleaders. People have become so entertained by the performance that when real worship enters the room, they don't know how to respond to it. Singing a slow gospel song is not worship. Exhorting and prompting the people to worship is not worship. These actions may happen in worship, but these things alone are not worship.

In St. Mark 11:23, after Jesus talks about speaking to the mountain and believing in faith, the latter part of that scripture says, *"he shall have whatsoever he saith."* Take a moment and think about the things you've said in the last thirty days. How did you respond when things didn't go as you planned? Did your conversation or declaration remain consistent and steadfast? Did your words reflect confidence that God will do whatever He said He would do? Oh, it sounds beautiful when we sing, *"God will do, what He said He will do. He's not a man that He should lie. He will come through."* (Fred Hammond, No Weapon). However, review what you said in the last 30 days when God's promises seemed slow and delayed. What does your worship sound like when life as you know it begins to fall apart around you? Are you still able to stand before

God's people on Sunday and sing down the heavens when your week has been absolute hell?

If we genuinely believe Proverbs 18:21 that says, *"death and life are in the power of the tongue,"* our conversations would be different. When life doesn't go as planned, instead of uttering things in frustration, we would speak more of what God says in His word. We would confess that we know God's promises will manifest in His set time. As worshippers, we must be attentive to what we say as we wait for God's blessings to come into fruition. It is crucial that we watch what we say! What conversations are you having when God gives you instructions that you don't understand or agree with? What are you saying when God tells you to sacrifice the thing you love? What do you say when God tells you to forgive the person who has wronged you? Your worship is tied to the words that come out of your mouth when there is no microphone in your hand. Do you want to be a worshipper?

Learn how to confess God's word in every situation and circumstance. Choose obedience over how you feel or what you think. No, it is not easy, but that is your reasonable sacrifice.So, worshipper, what will our heart's response be during times of tests and trials? Yes, Lord, yes - to Your will and to Your way. What will we do when nothing is going your way? I will exalt the Lord at all times, and His praises will continue to be in my mouth. What will be our response when life hits us where it hurts? Though He slay me, yet will I trust Him.

After all, this is what we say, profess, and encourage the people to do every Sunday. It's time that we begin to live out the words we say on Sunday. We can be a singer and a praise and worship leader by man's definition and standard. However, that does not make us worshippers. If we want to be worshippers, we must watch what we say with our mouths and our hearts, on and off the stage.

Take a moment and reflect on your life as a worshipper. Answer the following questions honestly.

What negative statements have you said lately? List them below.

_____

_____

_____

_____

_____

_____

_____

_____

What are you believing God for?

_____

_____

_____

_____

_____

_____

_____

_____

How do you respond when things don't go your way?

_____

_____

_____

_____

_____

_____

_____

_____

_____

After reading this chapter, what changes will you make in your life to ensure that you meet God's standard for being a true worshipper?

_____

_____

_____

_____

_____

_____

_____

_____

_____

Chapter Three

Actions Speak Louder Than Words

We've all heard the saying, *"Do as I say, not as I do."* Whether at home, school, or church, this saying is often said by those whose actions do not align with what they say, or how they expect others to act. In fact, by using this statement, one acknowledges that their actions do not align with what they claim to believe is appropriate. This is hypocrisy, and sadly, it is often exhibited from the classroom to boardrooms and everywhere in between. Hypocrisy anywhere is unpleasing in the eyes of God, however, the purpose of this book is not to address the hypocrisy of parents, preachers, and politicians, but rather those who claim to be worshippers.

Worshipper, let's ask ourselves this question, *Do I say one thing and do another?* In the last chapter, we took a look at the words that we allow our hearts and mouths to speak. However, it does not matter what we say if our actions don't align with it. If we declare and decree that we trust God, but when things don't go our way we ball up in fetal position and panic, our actions and speech contradict each other.

If we say that we believe God is a healer, but fear the outcomes of test results, our actions and speech contradict each other. Life happens to us all, saved and unsaved, rich and poor, good and bad. In fact, the Bible says in Matthew 5:45 (NIV), *"He causes his sun to rise on the evil and the good, and sends rain on the righteous and the unrighteous."* No matter who we are, we will experience rain and sunshine. The difference is how we respond. We chose how we will react to every situation that comes our way. We can decide to declare death and defeat, or we can press past what the flesh feels, sees, knows, and understands and choose life. Worshipper, what are our actions saying? Remember that people are watching our lives and listening to our declarations. Do our actions complement what's coming out of our mouth? Or, are we walking in hypocrisy?

It is an honor to lead God's people into praise and worship. Choosing individuals for this assignment should not be done without confirmation from God. Unfortunately, it is becoming increasingly common for church leadership to select a praise and worship leader based on skill and their ability to draw a crowd. Instead of asking the critical questions like, *"How are you living? What does your family, your co-workers, your neighbors, even your co-laborers in ministry say about your lifestyle?"* leaders are more concerned with the experience and notoriety of the individuals they select to lead praise and worship. Why is this becoming the norm? *Why is it allowed?*

1. **Gifts and callings are without repentance.** (Romans 11:29) Individuals can be gifted without the requirement of salvation, and God does not repent for giving the gift. Every person is born with gifts, and they have them even if they chose to misuse them, not use them, or refuse to use them to glorify God.

2. **There is a lack of discernment in many pulpits.** Discernment is ones ability to judge well. In the Christian context, it is the perception in the absence of judgment to obtain spiritual direction and

understanding. Where is the level of accountability for what worship has become in the house of God?

Worshippers, we are responsible for what worship has become in the house of God. If we are going to classify ourselves as worshippers, we have a responsibility to live the same life of holiness and confidence in God that we encourage others to live.

Take a moment and reflect on your life as a worshipper. Answer the following questions honestly.

Examine your life. Are there areas in which you are hypocritical? Think honestly and make notes of those areas below.

_____

_____

_____

_____

_____

_____

_____

_____

_____

_____

_____

_____

_____

_____

_____

_____

_____

Ask two friends that know you well to answer the following questions about you. Record their responses and what their responses revealed about you.

a. Do my actions align with my word?
b. How often do you see me operate in doubt or worry?

_____

_____

_____

_____

_____

_____

_____

_____

_____

_____

_____

_____

_____

_____

_____

_____

_____

After reading this chapter, what changes will you make in your life to ensure that you meet God's standard for being a true worshipper?

_____

_____

_____

_____

_____

_____

_____

_____

_____

_____

_____

_____

_____

_____

_____

_____

_____

_____

_____

Chapter Four

The Impact of a Worshipper

Our lives and decisions impact those connected to us. We often accept this truth when it comes to others reaping the benefit of seeing God bless us. However, we must examine what others are connected to in being a part of our lives and within our circle of influence.

We all have our imperfections. None of us are without our flaws and mistakes. Even those who strive to walk pleasing to God, love people, and live holy fall short at times. God never expects us to be perfect (flawless). However, when we miss the mark, He desires us to run to Him to get it right. We should all desire to be connected to like-minded individuals who refuse to willfully walk contrary to the Word of God.

We will struggle with areas in our flesh, however, when it is no longer a struggle, but our chosen way of life, it is a problem. Many people accept their struggles and expect others to accept them as just who they are. They say things like, *"This is who I am!"* or *"This is how God made me!"* On the contrary, the Bible says that God made us in His image and His likeness (Genesis 1:27). God was and is a holy God. We were made to be and live Holy as well! It's interesting how we will accept the creativeness, strength, and authority of God as a part of our DNA, however, when it comes to living holy, we create excuses to live otherwise.

Merriam-Webster defines struggle as *to proceed with difficulty or with great effort.* Can you think of some areas of your life that you are working on with *great effort?* Are there areas where you are struggling to change? If so, don't beat yourself up about them. The objective of this chapter is to be honest with ourselves about where we are. As defined by Merriam-Webster, the word *struggle* denotes action and a desire to change! That's the key – *a willingness to change!* After we admit that something is a struggle, we must refuse to use it as a crutch. Instead, we must fight to work through it and get to where God is calling us to be.

Sadly, we often classify things as struggles and make excuses when we want others to overlook what has now become sin in our lives. If we truly desire to change, we must be honest. Take a look at the areas in which you fall short. Are they really struggles? Are you adamant about working through them? Have you actually tried to deny your flesh in these areas? Are you seeking assistance? If not, it is likely that the things you've labeled as struggles are really bad habits.

If a praise and worship leader has an issue with alcohol abuse – *I'm not talking about "a little wine for the stomach's sake" (I Tim 5:23 KJV) or "be not drunk, wherein in excess" (Ephesians 5:18)* – I'm talking about getting tore up, staggering, stumbling drunk throughout the week and still be able to operate in the gift, lead praise and worship, and move the audience. Does this disqualify them as a praise and worship leader? There are two scenarios we must consider.

Scenario one If the individual is sorrowful and desires to be free from what has them bound. They are not disqualified as a worshipper. While they may need to take time away from their post to work through this issues, get poured into, and perhaps seek professional help, *they should not be disqualified as a worshipper.*

Scenario two With the same struggle, if the individual has no remorse, is not at all sorrowful, has no desire to change, and does not plan to stop, *this individual is disqualified to lead praise and worship.*

In the first example, we see a real struggle. This individual seeks wise counsel and is honest about their struggle. In the second example, however, the individual does not see an issue with their behavior. This is how we are able to detect the difference from a struggle and a chosen way of life. There were plenty of great men and women in the Bible who had struggles. In fact, many of them achieved great things for the glory of God in the middle of their struggles. Unfortunately, in many of our churches, especially when it comes to the discernment of who we allow to lead our congregations in praise and worship, many leaders could care less what their praise and worship leaders are doing. Their only concern is making sure that the people are moved enough by praise and worship to give good tithes and offering.

However, despite the church we serve in and the leadership we serve under, as a worshipper, we have a responsibility to God. Be honest. Do you see yourself in either of the scenarios above? Your issue may not be with alcohol, but what is your insight on your weakness? Is it truly a struggle, or have you made your sin a way of life?

Many people have a hard time confronting their flesh and being honest about their sin. We worry if others will demean us or overlook us. We wonder if our leaders will operate in the love of God found in Galatians 6 and *"restore such a one in the spirit of meekness, considering thyself, lest thou also be tempted."* In addition to church leadership that does not care, there are those who turn their backs on Christians who honestly struggle. So many do the complete opposite of what Paul admonishes us to do in Galatians 6. As a result, many worshippers find themselves in scenario two. They refuse to confess. They know the self- righteous, judgmental mothers, deacons, and bishops will ostracize and expose them. While the church must do better about seeing people as Jesus sees them, as a worshipper, we have a responsibility to ensure that we are in right standing with God.

Others are impacted greatly by our lives as worshippers. It goes far beyond what we do and say as we stand before the people with a mic in our hand. The minute we position ourselves as a worship leader, the eyes of the congregation are upon us. They will follow us on social media. They will look at the car we drive and the way we dress. They will desire to get to know us, where we shop, where we eat, how we treat others, and who we communicate with. Others are impacted not only by the service we render, but also the life we live. This impact can be positive or negative.

Does our daily life push people to live for God? Are our habits aligned with the Word of God? Will people see how we respond to trouble, slander, gossip, or even heartache and be encouraged to press through their various situations?

In Psalm 1:1, the Bible warns us of standing in the way of sinners. For some people, worshippers are the only example of God they will ever see. If we are saying (singing) one thing and doing (living) another, we could be responsible for someone not coming to God. Our actions could taint the way they see the body of Christ. As worshippers, we must consider if we are standing in the way of individuals coming to the Lord. Take a moment and think about how you are impacting the lives of others.

Take a moment and reflect on your life as a worshipper. Answer the following questions honestly.

Who are the individuals within your circle of influence?

_____

_____

_____

_____

_____

_____

_____

_____

_____

_____

_____

_____

_____

_____

_____

_____

_____

_____

_____

Select two of the individuals from your list and ask them to share how your life has impacted them. Next, take a moment and think about their response. Record the main parts of their response. Were you aware of your impact in their life? How can you be more intentional about your impact and influence? How does it make you feel to know that someone has been watching your life so closely?

_____

_____

_____

_____

_____

_____

_____

_____

_____

_____

_____

_____

_____

_____

_____

_____

After reading this chapter, what changes will you make in your life to ensure that you meet God's standard for being a true worshipper?

_____

_____

_____

_____

_____

_____

_____

_____

_____

_____

_____

_____

_____

_____

_____

_____

_____

_____

_____

_____

Chapter Five

You Are Responsible

As a worshipper, we have a responsibility to God, ourself, and God's people. Our responsibility to God is that we walk upright before Him. Walking upright before God requires us to spend time with Him in prayer and His Word so that we may come to know and understand how He wants us to live. Spending time with God is like being in a relationship with someone you love. The more time you spend with them, the more you learn about them. Remember, we can't worship what we do not know. We can't be a stranger to God and say we are worshipping Him. The more time we spend in the Word of God, the more He will transform our thinking. As our thinking is transformed, we will become more like God. As we become more like God, our life and the lives of those connected to us will transform. As a worshipper, the more time we spend with God, the more time we will want to spend with Him. Once we taste His presence, we will want to taste it again and again.

Worshipper, we are obligated to be honest with ourselves about where we are spiritually, mentally, and physically. Admit when you need help. Unfortunately, you cannot tell everyone in the church everything. James 5:16 (KJV) says, *"Confess your faults one to another, and pray one for another, that ye may be healed. The effectual fervent prayer of a righteous man availeth much."* Before you confess anything to anyone, be sure that the individual walks in righteousness and has a prayer life. We often believe that this scripture means to confess everything to everybody. However, James makes it clear that only the fervent prayers of a righteous man lead to breakthrough. It's impossible to pray fervently if we don't pray often. Someone with a real prayer life knows how to commune with God in intercession and pray through His will. Also, you will know a tree by the fruit it bears. Be sure to seek God when deciding to whom you will confess. Ask God to lead you to a wise and righteous individual who will pray with and for you and not blast your shortcomings in the church bulletin or worse – across the pulpit.

Finally, we have a responsibility to God's people. I minister in different places, and there are often people in attendance I don't know. Individuals have greeted me as if we've met and made reference to the setting in which we previous-ly met. As we discussed previously, when we stand on stage, we open our lives to people in ways we don't always fully perceive. It's impossible for us to know everyone we impact, but we must remember that we are impacting them. We won't know when they spot us and head in our direction to greet us. Sometimes, especially in public set-tings, a lot of time passes from when an individual spots us and when they make it to us. We can't be cursing out the cashier for overcharging us, yelling at the waiter for getting our order wrong, shouting at our kids for being hardheaded, or fussing with our significant other about personal issues.

Don't think that just because we represent God well in church settings that people won't be misled if they see us act out in public. We must be intentional about how we live away from the sanctuary, conference, or worship service. How many people have we injured or caused to stumble because of our double lives? We can't live one way when we're "on" in service but in a different setting be a completely different individual. Don't believe all the hype about "living your life for you." As leaders at the forefront, we have a responsibility to God's people. If you don't want it, it's probably best that you find something else to do for the Kingdom. This responsibility is there whether we acknowledge it or not. Why? Because God trusts us to lead His people. The Pastor isn't the only person responsible for the sheep. He/she shares this responsibility with every individual placed in front of the people to lead. People make an opinion about the church well before the Pastor gets up to preach. When we lead the congregation in praise and worship, we are trusted to lead the people into the presence of God. Once they get in His presence, their hearts are pricked, and they are moved to make changes in their lives.

Worshipper, we play just as much a part in people's lives as the pastor who delivers the word. If they see us in that light in church, but at Mardi Gras we are drunk and dancing in the streets, this could alter their understanding of what living for God truly means. It could make them believe that this is acceptable in God's house. Everyone does not understand that gifts come without repentance.

Some mistake talent for anointing and believe that anyone who can sing gospel well is living right. Many believe that living right is a prerequisite for being able to do anything good in God's house. While this should be the case, it is not always true. We all know people who can perform the house down, but live in sin. However, since the people we lead don't always understand this, we must be careful how we live on and off stage. Am I saying that we should put on a facade of holiness in public for people? No. I'm admonishing us to live holy – period. If we strive to live holy, we won't have to try to be holy when we are in public. God said, *"Be ye holy, for I am holy (I Peter 1:16, KJV).* As stated before, we all have areas in which we fall short. Many of our struggles keep us from upholding our obligations. In order to be able to work through these struggles and uphold our responsibility to God, ourselves, and God's people, we need more of God. Seeking more of God, desiring to go deeper in your relationship with God, or accessing a greater anointing does not come cheap.

When we make these requests, we should brace ourselves for the trials and seasons of suffering that will follow. If we expect to go deeper in worship, expect warfare to come our way. You see, Satan is a fallen angel. He was cast down from Heaven because he allowed pride to overtake him. He wanted to be greater than God. Don't think for a moment that he's going to sit back and let us draw nearer to God without sending all sorts of attacks our way. Please don't let this information about your adversary deter you from getting more of God. Understand that Satan can't do what he wants to do in your life. When you belong to God, the enemy has to get permission from God to test you. God permits it because He knows the tests, trials, and temptations of the enemy will draw you closer to Him as you requested in the first place. So, worshipper, when hell hits your life in the worst way, tell your enemy, "Thanks." Know that the storms you have to endure will equip you to uphold your responsibility to God, yourself, and God's people.

Take a moment and reflect on your life as a worshipper. Answer the following questions honestly.

Outside of church, how much time do you spend with God? How do you spend this time in His presence?

_____

_____

_____

_____

_____

_____

_____

How well do you uphold your obligations to God's people?

_____

_____

_____

_____

_____

_____

_____

_____

Can you identify the areas in which you struggle? What are you doing to overcome these struggles?

After reading this chapter, what changes will you make in your life to ensure that you meet God's standard for being a true worshipper?

_____

_____

_____

_____

_____

_____

_____

_____

_____

_____

_____

_____

_____

_____

_____

_____

_____

_____

_____

_____

Chapter Six

My Life Is Not
My Own

n Ephesians 3:1 (KJV), Paul refers to himself as a *prisoner of the Lord Jesus*. When we think of a prisoner, we think of one who has been stripped of their freedom. We think of someone who has no choice other than to do what those in authority tell them to do. Paul classifies himself as being stripped of the freedom to do what he wants to do. He declares that He is a prisoner to the authority of Jesus Christ.

As a worshipper, do you consider yourself a prisoner to the Lord Jesus Christ? Do you live your life as one who belongs to the Lord? When people see and hear you outside of the church can they tell that you belong to God? Does your speech betray you as Peter's did when he tried to deny being one of Jesus' disciples? (Matthew 26:69-74). In those few verses, Peter denied Jesus three times. How many times have you denied the Lord? How often has someone seen you outside of church doing something that was not becoming of a worshipper? As worshippers, we don't belong to ourselves. William McDowell pinned a compelling song that took the world by storm entitled, *I Give Myself Away*. We all know it. Many of us sing it in our services weekly. Some of the lyrics to the song say,

> *"My life is not my own. To you, I belong. I give myself; I give myself to you."*

These lyrics are powerful – until we have to live it! When we sing this song, we declare that our lives aren't ours. We declare that we belong to God. We declare that we give (and continue to give) ourselves to Him. If we truly believe this, then we know that we cannot live any way we please. Prisoners don't decide what time they eat, sleep, or talk to others. They don't make choices, and they can't negotiate the decisions made for them. Again, are you a prisoner of the Lord Jesus Christ? Is He the authority on all things in every area of your life?

Once we proclaim to be a worshipper, there is a lifestyle of accountability we must live up to. Many of us despise accountability and are therefore unfit to call ourselves worship leaders. We don't like having to report or explain ourselves to others. We want to walk in service 5 minutes late or even worse, not show for prayer and then just be "on" when it's time to sing. As worshippers, we must submit to accountability. It's not just for us; it's also for those we lead. Many of us could have a better impact as worshippers if we would simply allow ourselves to be held accountable.

Additionally, worshippers are disciplined. In his 2011 blog, "Becoming a Disciplined Person," Todd Smith, opens the blog with the following statement:

"Self-discipline is a pattern of behavior where you choose to do what you know you should do, rather than what you want to do. It's the inner power that pushes you to get out of bed to exercise rather than sleeping in."

Just as we discipline ourselves to practice, we must discipline ourselves to pray, fast, and deny our flesh. Living for God isn't always as easy as we believe it to be. The temptations of the enemy are things that our flesh desires. Yes, the Bible tells us to resist temptation, and the enemy will flee. However, resistance and discipline fall hand in hand. It takes discipline to deny sex when you know God desires you to wait until you are married. It takes discipline to refrain from cursing someone out after they've been rude. It takes discipline to practice when you know you're gifted and can finesse well. Though it is a tough muscle to build, discipline is vital in the lives of worshippers. When we take the stand as worshippers, we must accept that our lives no longer belong to us. Accountability and discipline are key to living as prisoners to Jesus Christ.

Take a moment and reflect on your life as a worshipper. Answer the following questions honestly.

List the areas in your life that you have not surrendered to God. State why you haven't released these areas to Him.

_____

_____

_____

_____

_____

_____

_____

_____

_____

_____

_____

_____

_____

_____

_____

_____

_____

How do you respond to being held accountable for your actions as a worship leader? Why do you chose to respond this way? How can you better honor and submit to the accountability (leaders, mentors, pastors) in your life?

After reading this chapter, what changes will you make in your life to ensure that you meet God's standard for being a true worshipper?

_____

_____

_____

_____

_____

_____

_____

_____

_____

_____

_____

_____

_____

_____

_____

_____

_____

_____

_____

_____

_____

Chapter Seven

To Sing or Not to Sing

As we discussed previously, there are many forms of worship. In this particular chapter, we will deal with the form of singing. Let's ask ourselves this question, *Are we worshippers or are we singers?* Yes, there is a difference. Plenty of people can sing, and possess pure talent and skill. Others, some of which may not be the "best" singers, will worship God and you will feel it and know that a worshipper has entered the building.

Think about the last worship service, conference, or service you were in. What did praise and worship sound and look like? What do you remember about it? I recall being at an event where several ministries were represented by their praise teams and soloists. Though this was a while ago, I can still remember how I felt when a particular individual mounted the platform and opened her mouth. It was more than a good or a nice sound. It was more than the words or the arrangements of the songs she sang. Her worship came from her heart. It was pure, authentic, and genuine. The sound was rich. It was full, and it had depth. When was the last time you heard or felt that when someone led praise and worship or ministered in song? Why is this not the norm but rather the exception?

Singing is an art. It can be taught and improved over time through practicing. It is rehearsed, which is why we have rehearsals or practice. Worship, on the other hand, can't be rehearsed or practiced. It happens organically. It is not drummed up. Real worship invades rehearsal when true worshippers get together. I have been in rehearsals where the very presence of God was invoked and invited in. Rehearsal quickly became a worship experience. We have to seize every worship opportunity afforded to us in a corporate setting – whether it's a church service or a choir rehearsal. I have been in praise team and choir rehearsals, even a workshop where before the end of it, the atmosphere shifted to worship. You know why? There were like- minded-people with hearts toward God who didn't mind yielding their will, agenda, and schedules to God's will. Why isn't this the norm? John 4:23 (KJV) says, *"But the hour cometh, and now is, when the true worshippers shall worship the Father in spirit and in truth: for the Father seeketh such to worship him."* Who is the *such*? Those who will worship God in spirit and in truth. There's no other way to experience God – period!

I love to hear good singing just as much as the next person. However, if we're going to experience God, we have to press past good singing. Sometimes, it can turn into performances and competitions in an attempt to get a response from the crowd. What about God's response? Look, there is no time for being entertained in the house of God. It's okay to want to enjoy service and even have a good time with other believers, but this cannot be all we look forward to in the house of God. People are dealing with real issues, and they need real answers. The only way we're going to get those answers is from God in worship. It's going to require more than a good arrangement for strongholds to break, families to be restored, and bodies to be healed. It's going to take people who are tired of the flesh dominating our worship services; people who are willing to sacrifice their time and their own desires; people who will seek God so that they can hear what it is He has to say – not only to them individually – but to the body of Christ collectively. This will require sacrifice.

Remember, worship is not just about how we feel. True worship will require us to forsake our desires, press past our pain, and put aside our own trials and tribulations. Worship is an act of obedience and faith.

Take a moment and reflect on your life as a worshipper. Answer the following questions honestly.

Think back on a true worship experience you had in a corporate setting. What did it feel like? What made it "true worship" to you?

_____

_____

_____

_____

_____

_____

_____

_____

_____

_____

_____

_____

_____

_____

_____

_____

Recall a moment in which you had to press through difficult circumstances to worship? How did you feel afterwards? What did you do to press through your feelings?

_____

_____

_____

_____

_____

_____

_____

_____

_____

_____

_____

_____

_____

_____

_____

_____

_____

_____

After reading this chapter, what changes will you make in your life to ensure that you meet God's standard for being a true worshipper?

_____

_____

_____

_____

_____

_____

_____

_____

_____

_____

_____

_____

_____

_____

_____

_____

_____

_____

Chapter Eight

There's No "A" In Worship

W-O-R-S-H-I-P, that's how you spell *worship*. When you think of worship or more particularly, a worshipper, what visual image comes to mind? Your answer will depend on what you've been taught about worship – what it is, how it sounds and yes, even how it looks. Some of us have minimized worship to the tempo of a song and synthesized chords on a keyboard. While that may be the case in some worship moments – *it's so much more than that*.

Let's do this exercise together: Close your eyes and take a deep breath. Now, think of worship. See yourself in a worship service. Visualize the individual or individuals standing before the congregation leading praise and worship. What does it sound like? What does it look it? How do they look? I'm not talking about outer appearances. How are they positioned spiritually? What do their hearts sound like? Keep your eyes closed and listen carefully. What do you hear? Is it a soft, soothing, ministering sound of love, peace, gratefulness, and appreciation? Open your eyes. What it should not sound like is ARROGANCE! There is no "A" in worship. There's no place for arrogance in worship.

I am always amazed when those of us who call ourselves worshippers are loving and humble during service but mean and arrogant when we get off the stage. Why are some "worshippers" like this? It's not that they are too busy to be kind. Or even that they are still "in the spirit." The truth is, some of those claiming to be worshippers are incredibly talented, and that's where the ball stops.

They have no real relationship with God, so there's no real change in our lives. There is no fruit of love or kindness in our interactions with others. Some people allow their gift and talents to keep them from showing the love of Christ beyond the stage. If we are not careful, many of our gifts and talents will lead us straight to hell. Yes, it is possible to lift your eyes in hell even though you've spent your life leading praise and worship every Sunday. (See Matthew 7:22).How do these type of people gain access to God's people? When church leaders become more concerned with the performance of a praise and worship leader rather than their life, our altars, pulpits, and stages become stained with arrogant worship leaders. Some pastors have no idea of how the praise and worship leader is living – yes, the one on their payroll – and they don't care! Their only concern is building a ministry and making themselves look good.

Again, worshippers, you have a responsibility to ensure that you check yourself for behaviors that are not pleasing to God. Even if your pastor or leader never checks you for being prideful and arrogant, you still have a responsibility of taking inventory of your actions.

Arrogance is a subtle little spirit. It creeps in without you even realizing it sometimes. When you are good at what you do, people will compliment you. While it feels great to know you are appreciated, you must be so careful not to let accolades be the motivation behind what you claim you are doing for God.

Though He often left people in awe, Jesus never operated in arrogance.He always strived to please God. He often informed those He influenced that everything He did, He did through the Father. St. John 8:29 (KJV) says, *"And he that sent me is with me: the Father hath not left me alone; for I do always those things that please him."* As a worshipper, is this your testimony as well? Is your heart's desire to please God with your worship as well as your life?

Arrogance is not an attribute of the spirit of God. It has no place in the lives or hearts of worshippers. We must pray and ask God to purge all filthiness of the flesh from us. We have to stay in a posture of prayer, remain humble, and understand that whenever He chooses to use us — it's all Him and absolutely none of us! I love the song, *This is the Air I Breathe*. It reminds me that I can't even breathe until and unless God breathes the very breath of life in me. When we realize that, it should humble us and keep us in a place of thanksgiving. It should remind us that God chose us, not because of us, but in spite of us.

W-O-R-S-H-I-P – there's no "A" in worship!

Take a moment and reflect on your life as a worshipper. Answer the following questions honestly.

Have you ever experienced an arrogant person? What was your experience like with this individual?

_____

_____

_____

_____

_____

_____

_____

_____

_____

_____

_____

_____

_____

_____

_____

_____

_____

_____

_____

Where do you need to humble yourself? List the areas in your life where unidentified arrogance may be lying dormant.

_____

_____

_____

_____

_____

_____

_____

_____

_____

_____

_____

_____

_____

_____

_____

_____

_____

_____

_____

_____

After reading this chapter, what changes will you make in your life to ensure that you meet God's standard for being a true worshipper?

_____

_____

_____

_____

_____

_____

_____

_____

_____

_____

_____

_____

_____

_____

_____

_____

_____

_____

_____

Chapter Nine

Worship is a Way of Life

Well, worshippers, we've made it to the final chapter. I pray that the previous chapters have been a blessing to you. Also, I pray that you've developed a true understanding of what it means to be a worshipper. I wrote this book, not to demean, but to cause worshippers to look within themselves. Very often, as worshippers, we spend a lot of time ensuring that everyone around us is pleased. Sometimes, we are encouraged to go against what we feel in our spirit just to appease those who have employed us. Many times, we go home filling empty because we've been pulled on in every facet. Sometimes, we have to usher in the spirit as others are prayed for, receive deliverance, and hear prophecy for their lives. We are often overlooked because of our operation during high moments in service.

As a worshipper, I get it, and I understand. The weight of this assignment is sometimes very heavy, but know that with the help of God, you can carry out your assignment in the earth. Honestly, many of the things the Holy Spirit led me to write about in this book even convicted me. It was through this conviction that I learned the very first step to receiving the help we need in any circumstance. Being honest. The truth is, no matter how good our lives look on the outside, no one has it all figured out. We walk life by faith and nothing except the grace of God allows us to still live through our mistakes. Being a worshipper does not mean you will be exempt from tests, trials, suffering or pain. This is life, and it matters not whether you are saved or unsaved; you will experience life.

If you've served God for any length of time, you know that life is a mixture of good and bad experiences. Our hope is not in having a perfect and comfortable life, but rather in knowing that all things work together for the good of them who love the Lord. (Romans 8:28). When we go through difficulties and the weapons are formed against us, it is natural to wonder if God sees us and hears our prayers. As worshippers, we must be able to tap into the power of God within us. Worship responds to what we would define as a negative human experience from a supernatural level. This is not something you can just do on Sunday morning. This must be a part of who you are. This must be your lifestyle. True worship works wonders. It can stop us from making fleshly decisions. It keeps us sane when we are going through things that should have left us crazy. Worship reminds us of how great God is even when He allows us to go through things that hurt.

As we lead others in worship, let us remember to live what we sing about. Sure, it sounds great to sing about persevering, enduring, and withstanding without complaining, but what happens when we actually have to live it?

Songs of victory sound great on Sunday morning when we're worshipping together. But will you remember your victory when you are faced with a trial on Monday, and there is no organ, microphone, or bass player in sight? Worship should not only be what we do. It should be who we are. Heaven and Hell should respond when *worshippers* worship. Sickness should bow when *worshippers* worship. Miracles and healing should flow when *worshippers* worship. These should not be moments we experience periodically in worship. It should be the norm for the worshipper.

As worshippers, we will be tried by people and unfair situations. In the midst of all of this, we must choose to worship as we allow God to fight our battles. Even as I write this book, I am waiting for God to settle some situations on my behalf. As I wait, *I worship*. Yes, it sometimes seems quicker to handle things on our own. We may even believe (with our carnal mind) that our actions would be justified. However, as worshippers, we must choose to operate from a different dimension. We must choose to worship and wait on God. Know, without a shadow of doubt, that God will avenge you and fix the situation. God has a track record with us. His resume is flawless. He has never failed us. Though He rarely comes when we want Him to, His timing is always perfect. When it seems that He is slow in coming, change your perspective in worship! As a worshipper, remember that it is an honor and a privilege to be trusted by God to lead His people into praise and worship, no matter the place or platform. Despite our attempts at holiness, we are still unworthy of this privilege. None of us have arrived. Every day we *"press toward the mark for the prize of the high calling of God in Christ Jesus."* (Philippians 3:14, KJV). It takes effort every day.

As worshippers, we must understand that without God, we're not effective. We're just entertaining. I don't know about you, but I want my worship to touch the very heart of God. We should desire Him to sit in our worship like He's sitting beside us in a room. Our love for God should push us to live a life that is pleasing to Him. Yes, there are many sacrifices we must make as worshippers. With God's help, we will make them.

Worshippers, we have enough good singers in church. God's people need kingdom-minded worshippers who can invoke the presence of God when they open their mouths. This is what every worshipper should desire. We should pray that people feel God every time we open our mouths to minister. This requires sacrifice.

So, you say you want to be a worshipper? What sacrifices are you willing to make to be the worshipper God is calling for in this season? How bad do you want it? If you don't remember anything else I've shared, please remember this: *Worship extends far past Sunday morning. Worship is a lifestyle!* What does your lifestyle say about worship?

About the Author

Wife. Mother. Gospel Recording Artist. Entrepreneur, First Lady and now, Author! These are words that describe Gail Fly. A native of New Orleans, Louisiana, Gail was raised in church and developed a love for gospel music at an early age. She was drawn to praise and worship and became the praise and worship leader in several ministries. She is an award-winning independent gospel recording artist and President of Raising the Standard Music, LLC, an independent gospel music label, building a platform for independent gospel artists. Of all of her accomplishments and the roles she fills in life; wife and mother are her most rewarding. Gail believes and as a First Lady, teaches, "our first ministry is to our families!" Gail is married to Pastor Albert E. Fly, Sr., pastor of Raising the Standard Ministries in New Orleans, LA. They are the proud parents of Albert E. Fly, Jr.

Stay Connected

Thank you for reading So You Want To Be A Worshipper. Gail looks forward to connecting with you and keeping you updated on her next releases. Below are a few ways you can connect with the author.

Facebook GailFlytheAuthor
Instagram bgailfly
Twitter GailFly
Website www.gailfly.com

Made in the USA
Middletown, DE
08 March 2022

62335218R00052